ACTIVATE TO ACHIEVE

The 411 On Refocusing To Overcome A Self-Sabotaging Mindset And Emerge Successful

Shackeria D. Mesquita

ACTIVATE TO ACHIEVE. Copyright © 2021. Shackeria D. Mesquita. All Rights Reserved.

Printed in the United States of America.

No portion of this book may be reproduced, stored in a retrieval system, or transmitted in any form or by any means, except for brief quotations in printed reviews, without the prior written permission of DayeLight Publishers or Shackeria D. Mesquita.

Published by

DayeLight PUBLISHERS

ISBN: 978-1-953759-49-8 (paperback)

Scripture quotations marked (NIV) are taken from the Holy Bible, New International Version®, NIV®. Copyright © 1973, 1978, 1984 by Biblica, Inc.™ Used by permission of Zondervan. All rights reserved worldwide.

Scripture quotations marked (NLT) are taken from the Holy Bible, New Living Translation, copyright © 1996, 2004, 2007 by Tyndale House Foundation. Used by permission of Tyndale House Publishers, Inc., Carol Stream, Illinois 60188. All rights reserved.

Scripture quotations marked "NKJV" are taken from the New King James Version. Copyright © 1982 by Thomas Nelson, Inc. Used by permission. All rights reserved. Bible text from the New King James Version® is not to be reproduced in copies or otherwise by any means except as permitted in writing by Thomas Nelson, Inc., Attn: Bible Rights and Permissions, P.O. Box 141000, Nashville, TN 37214-1000.

Scripture quotations marked "ESV" are from the ESV Bible® (The Holy Bible, English Standard Version®), copyright © 2001 by Crossway Bibles, a publishing ministry of Good News Publishers. Used by permission. All rights reserved.

Dedication

This book is dedicated to my father, Danavan Mesquita, and my uncle, Rodney Austin. I was blessed with an earthly father as well as an uncle who was also like a father to me. I love you both, and I will always remember to do my best, as that is all you ever required of me.

Acknowledgments

I give God thanks for venturing into the wilderness to find me. I am grateful for the purpose He has entrusted to me, paired with my gifts and talents that have helped me to grow, develop and impact others. I give Him glory and honour as I wrote this first book. I relied on Him, and He was never busy.

To my father and brother, Danavan Mesquita Senior and Junior, who accommodated me reading the book's draft to them almost every week, I say thank you. They believed in my capability and encouraged me to share my journey so I can help others who were going through the same thing. My gratitude is extended especially to my daddy for raising me the best way he could and teaching me life lessons and the power of not giving up.

To my stepmother, Carolyn Chin, who stepped in and played the role of mother to an almost adult me, not leaving me to chance and thinking that I was beyond change, love always. Thank you for always being there during my sleepless nights and for creating happy moments.

To my cheerleaders, the race is not for the swift but for who can endure. "You are a fighter!" "Be courageous in your service" and "I am proud of you" are just some things they would say to keep me going. Thank you, Lord, for being selective with my encounters and interaction.

To every person I have come in contact with, whether for a short or long period of time, I thank you because you have contributed to my growth and development.

Table of Contents

Dedication 5

Acknowledgments... 7

Introduction 11

Chapter One: The Right Attitude 13

    What Kind Of Attitude Do You Have? 19

    The Doubtful Attitude 20

    The 'Go-Getter' Attitude.................................... 21

    Gratitude Attitude.. 22

Chapter Two: Set Your Goals 27

Chapter Three: Positioning Yourself................... 33

Chapter Four: Persistence, Consistency, And Discipline Combo.. 39

Chapter Five: Focus 45

Chapter Six: Reflection 51

Chapter Seven: How To Self-Introspect 55

Quotes and Affirmation For Self Activation..... 61
Author's Final Message 71
About The Author 73

Introduction

We all chase success, and a lot of us have a problem with not achieving anything or as much as we can. We then try quick-fix tips and strategies. When they do not work, we say motivational speakers, coaches, and inspirational authors are frauds. The reality is, we are approaching these tips and strategies deactivated; all that good advice received is not utilized because you are not in a state of mind to use it to your advantage. So, let us explore some of the things that prevented me and may be preventing you from achieving. In this book, I highlight, through the practice of reflection, areas in our lives that we need to pay attention to if we want to be activated so we can be successful at anything we desire.

At this stage, let us just get an understanding of what self-activation is. Self-activation is a mental state of being which manifests in the physical. It is a process

Shackeria D. Mesquita

where YOU are triggered to succeed because YOU recognize that YOU hold the key to fail or achieve.

Chapter One

The Right Attitude

"Attitude is a little thing that makes a big difference." —Winston Churchill

We have always heard the saying that "Your attitude determines your altitude," but is this true? If you do not understand what is meant by attitude, before you read any further, reflect on a scenario where you approached a situation with optimism. Now do the same with a situation where you had a negative approach. What did you discover? Do you agree with the saying, "Your attitude determines your altitude" after that reflective exercise? Through my daily reflective exercise, I realized how much or how little I achieved on my journey because of my attitude. Therefore, it was only right for me to start by pointing out just how important having a positive attitude is to acquiring and maintaining success.

Attitude is something a lot of us pay little attention to. Churchill made a great point that though attitude is a small thing, it makes a huge difference in our relationship with others and how much we achieve in our lifetime. If Churchill is right, and I do believe he is, then it is important to pay attention to our way of thinking and our feelings towards the people and things around us.

The reality is, our thoughts are a part of us, and they manifest in our actions, whether we do or do not do something. We, in turn, call it luck or bad luck, depending on the response we get. As an educator, I tell my students that their attitude goes beyond the rolling of the eyes, the craning of the neck, and all the other body languages, which are just physical evidence of what is really happening inside their heads. Through that concept, I came to realize that mindset is everything.

Irving Berlin said, "Attitudes are a secret power working twenty-four hours a day, for good or bad. It is of paramount importance that we know how to harness and control this great force." Attitude starts in the mind, so our mindset can make or break us. Therefore, we must be careful what we feed our minds. I was once told that what we feed will grow. What are we downloading in our minds? What are we connecting to our minds? We have to decide if our mindset will be positive or negative. Yes, we must choose; it is one of our God-given gifts after all—a positive mindset yields tremendous benefits, which will be highlighted throughout this book.

Now, life is not all sunshine and rainbow. We may encounter undesirous situations ever so often, and it is our reaction that determines how we overcome these situations. This reaction is based on how our mind is trained to function. Is your mind trained to be optimistic or pessimistic? The process our minds go through during the time of the situation is manifested in our actions towards the situation. I believe the mind is capable of getting me through anything I am faced with once it is trained to be positive.

Many of us do not trust our minds or intuition: your gut feeling. We approach situations based on the experiences of others, not realizing that even though we are all a part of the book of life, we all have our own chapters and episodes. Nothing is wrong with seeking advice and being coached. I have done all of that myself, but having to resort to self-motivation very early in life, I consult the mind first. I was not always like that though; I had to go through the process of mind renewal.

Through mind renewal, I changed the diet for my mind and became activated. That is how I started trusting my mind and changing my attitude towards situations and the choices I make. I believe our choices determine where we end up. So, we have to now decide if our destination or success is based on our attitude or the attitude of others. No matter how good an adviser your friends are, no matter how many coaching sessions you invest in, no matter how many empowerment events you attend, if you are deactivated, then you cannot manifest into greatness. Remember, it is an awareness that leads to actions. As **Scottie Waves** says, "Think for yourself. Trust your own intuition. Another's mind isn't walking your journey, you are." So, are you going to listen to your mind, which says, "Let us try" or the people who say, "It is impossible?"

When I became activated, I realized my mindset needed tuning. I was able to dream, but I was doubtful. Mentally I was one of my worst enemies because I believed all the negative things that were said about me, so I failed to disappoint my critics. Even when there was no doubt I could or would achieve something, I downplayed my value; self-sabotage is a monster. Mind renewal helped me to stop allowing the negative downpour of others, fear, and self-doubt that I was not good enough to stop me from achieving.

Did I tell you I was not always positive or successful? I was far from it. I have been tied up in my mind, and I listened to the congregation who met in my head on a daily basis, numerous times for the day too. They would tell me and convince me that I was not qualified, I was too weak, or it required years of service, which I did not have, and the list went on. That got me NOWHERE! My mind had an imbalanced diet; it was suffering from malnutrition—too much of one thing is not good. I fed on, "I can't" until I screamed, "I can't do this anymore." Being nowhere and in a state of nothingness was depressing, and I needed out; my appetite needed an upgrade. I had to let go and let GOD. He introduced me to alone time. I needed to get away from the crowd in order to survive. I was unable to listen to the voices around me because to them, I was not good enough, and that was junk food for my mind.

In the tenth grade, I was told I would not be anything in life. I believed those things, so I needed to be separated from those who thought nothing of me. I pulled away from the crowd and started feeding my mind with positive words and messages from books, music, speeches, and documentaries. No one said to me, "Oh, read this, listen this or watch that." It was inspiration, and I credit God for that. I then came to the conclusion that sometimes we need to step back to make the best steps forward. It seemed like I was alone, but God was with me and provided inspiration all the way.

As a woman of faith, a believer in God, I had to turn to one of my refocus lessons which was **Isaiah 41:10 (NKJV), "Fear not, for I am with you; be not dismayed, for I am your God; I will strengthen you, I will help you, I will uphold you with my righteous right hand."** This scripture was like a supplement for me. After reading it, my attitude was like that of a champion, overcoming doubts and fear because I have the best person in my corner. I do not need to focus on past stressful experiences and people's negative opinions regarding the mission ahead.

Hans Selye said, "Adopting the right attitude can convert a negative stress into a positive one." I am a living example of this. After being told I would amount to nothing by an educator, months later, my father was told that I would no longer be accommodated at that school, so he must consider enrolling me elsewhere. I felt rejected yet again because thirteen years prior, my mother had turned me over to my father at age two so she could go and live her life. *I must be defective*, were my thoughts, but I had an awakening because of reflection. I reflected on the teacher telling me I would amount to nothing and my dad saying, "prove him wrong." Initially, it sounded like the silliest thing, and it did not happen overnight, but my negative situation turned out okay because I reflected on it, and my attitude was, *"Who told him he got to decide where and how I ended up?"* That was me being positive. I was now in a state of activation.

What Kind Of Attitude Do You Have?

Understanding the type of attitude we have can help us to improve ourselves and reap success. Be mindful that we do not go through life alone. We encounter hundreds, if not thousands of people along the journey to success, whether in person or on social media. Our attitude towards ourselves, others, and situations will determine how far we reach, how much we achieve, and how long it takes to actually achieve. I will discuss the various attitudes I have learned from observing myself and the people around me.

The Doubtful Attitude

"Your living is determined not so much by what life brings to you as by the attitude you bring to life; not so much by what happens to you as by the way your mind looks at what happens." —**Kahlil Gibran**

Most times, we are our own stumbling blocks because of the thoughts we harbour about ourselves and the situations we find ourselves in. A job offer may pop up, and our response is, "I am not good enough for that role; I have never done this before; could God really use me for that?" and the list goes on. A doubtful attitude will put you a couple of steps behind, maybe too many steps behind, or you might just lose the opportunity entirely. During a devotional exercise in my first year at teachers' college, one of our Vice Principals shared a story about her time studying. She said she needed financial help to complete her studies, and it just so happened that a scholarship was on the table, but it was not for her faculty. Whether it was for her faculty or not, she did not make that stop her, and the greatest thing was that she did not allow doubt to hinder her, so she applied. Now whether she got that scholarship or not leads us to another type of attitude.

The 'Go-Getter' Attitude

"The greatest discovery of all time is that a person can change his future by merely changing his attitude." —**Oprah Winfrey**

I strongly believe in mind renewal and transformation. I grew up watching Ian Boyne's show 'Profile,' so from early on I knew that not all great men got a good head start; some started out homeless and had their ideas rejected numerous times, but that did not stop them. But what I always wondered was, what was the driving force behind their persistence? I got the answer in early 2018 while in a taxi. I must add that if it was not for introspection, I would not have found the answer. So, a young man stopped the taxi I was in one morning and told the driver he had no taxi fare. The driver decided to take him to his destination nonetheless. I admired the driver's kindness. I then looked at the young man's attire and remembered where he told the driver he was going. I asked if he was going for an interview, and he said, "No, work." I later realized he was a trainee. My mind started turning, and I remembered that where we picked him up, there were no houses nearby as the nearest community to that road was a good distance away. I surmised that he either hitched a ride or he walked that lonely road in the early morning, and that is when I got my answer to how all those interviewed on Profile and my now transformed-self did it: 'ATTITUDE.' We had to get there; therefore, by any cost, we got there. We had to get out of our comfort zone and ask for favours like that young man that morning. We had to feed our minds with positivity and develop good habits which yielded great results and success.

There are persons in life who are successful because of the final attitude I want to share.

Gratitude Attitude

No matter the size of the deed, always show appreciation because if you had it or could have done it, Mr. Good Deed would not have needed to step in. My greatest gratitude is to God. If it were not for Him, I would not have gotten help from some of the most unlikely persons, and I would not have made some of my best decisions; this book is one of them.

The gratitude attitude is simple: appreciation. It is important to know that attitude can be heard, seen, and felt. Can you imagine losing assistance or an opportunity because of ungratefulness? Try to develop an attitude of gratitude. Say "thank you" to everyone for everything they do for you and be genuine too. **2 Corinthians 9:13-14 (NLT)** tells us, "As a result of your ministry, men will give glory to God. For your generosity to them and to all believers, will prove that you are obedient to the Good News of Christ. And they will pray for you with deep affection because of the overflowing grace God has given to you." We are nothing, and we do nothing without God. So whatever greatness God has allowed another human being to do for us, He will be glorified. Their deed is evidence of obedience to God, who directed them to help, even when you did not ask them for help. I believe from experience that this level of gratitude expands our blessings and opportunities. It pays to have a gratitude attitude.

Activating any one of these attitudes comes with consequences and rewards. Being doubtful feeds fear and procrastination. Having a mindset to go and get what is yours and being grateful throughout the process is and will be one of the most fulfilling feelings you could ever have.

Having a good attitude is crucial. We need to think that as we live, we are under a large microscope that anyone can use at any time to view who they choose, and that person may just be you.

Often we do not realize we are placed in a situation, and we do not realize that we have an audience with an opportunity or access to an opportunity we have been longing for. It is at that moment our nonchalant, non-ambitious, self-sabotaging attitude reveals its ugly head. It could be that you have a task to execute, and your lack of effort or care in getting the task done is evident. It could also be that you had to work with someone and treated the person poorly, disregarding their opinions, being disrespectful, or using them for your gain. Whatever the scenario, a potential employer may just see that and disregard you completely, thinking to themselves, "Now that is not a person I want on my team." **Ephesians 4:29 (NKJV)** says, "Let no corrupt word proceed out of your mouth, but what is good for necessary edification, that it may impart grace to the hearers." I have added action to that, so be careful of your speech and actions in situations so that people who are witnesses in the moment are pleased with your attitude. A bad attitude can literally block love, blessings, and destiny from finding you. Do not be the reason you do not succeed. A positive attitude has ripple effects: positive thoughts lead to positive actions, ensuing positive results. A positive attitude changes everything. It can brighten a gloomy atmosphere and even turn things in your favour. Remember, a great attitude becomes a great mood, which becomes a great day, which becomes a great year, which becomes an extraordinarily great life.

"You cannot have a positive life and a negative mind." —**Joyce Meyer**

Consider the equations $-2+1 = -1$ and $1+-2= -1$. In both equations, the results are negative; no matter the position of the negative number, the result is negative. Whether we are upfront with our negativity or we mask it, it will be revealed in our fruitless results. No one wants to receive a negative result. I am in total agreement with Meyer; there is no way you can have a positive life with a negative attitude.

A lot of affluent men and women are not respected because of their attitude, and this eventually affects their brands and business ventures. So, it does not matter your purpose, just ensure your attitude is positive.

Chapter Two

Set Your Goals

"One secret to success is setting goals." —Author Unknown

Do you want to be successful? Well, you have to plan for it. You have to plan to work and plan to receive the success when it comes because it needs to be maintained for future opportunities. One of the biggest secrets to success is setting goals. It is possibly one of the most shared secrets that a lot of people fail to run with. If I had researched and actively jumped on this secret earlier, without a doubt, I would have made better choices and could have possibly reached further in life. You see, procrastination is single-handedly our worse enemy, and he was my friend; he was not a good friend, might I add. I had so many ideas, dreams, plans, whatever you may call them, and they amounted to nothing. On my journey of mind renewal, I learned a lot about the process of goal setting and just how effective it is if activated and not just left in our minds. I believe knowledge is wealth if used correctly, and so I will share some of my life lessons and what I do.

Lesson 1: When setting my goals, I am specific. I identify exactly what I want to accomplish. Ensure they are measurable; I am then able to assess myself, the method, and the progress I am making to reach my goals. Your goals need to be attainable; whether they are simple or challenging, they should be winnable. Why set your basket where you cannot reach it? Sometimes we have dreams that are just fairy tales, wishful thinking.

Your goals should be realistic and sensible. They should be representational and convincing; that way you can sell the idea and get help because there may come a time when you need a hand bigger and stronger than yours. Is your goal for personal benefit, community development, or is it a benefit to the country's economy? If your answer is no to any of those, what is the point of the goal then? Your goal needs to be relevant. What purpose will it serve to you or society?

A goal must have an endpoint where you are satisfied you have accomplished that goal. It is important to have a time and date when you hope to meet this goal. Being time-bound helps to keep you focused and driven to accomplish whatever goals you set. If you followed closely, you would have realized I am a big fan of using the SMART acronym to set goals. While they are smart, they should also make you want to jump out of bed in the morning and be excited about success.

Lesson 2: "…Write the vision; make it plain on tablets, so he may run who reads it. For still the vision awaits its appointed time; it hastens to the end—it will not lie. If it seems slow, wait for it; it will surely come; it will not delay." (**Habakkuk 2:2-3 - ESV)**. This is what the good book tells us about setting goals.

I am a visual learner, so I could not depend on my mind only; it keeps shifting so the ideas go. Because I wanted my ideas to remain and be visible, I got into the habit of journaling and creating vision boards. When I decided to write this book, I wrote down specific objectives; for example, the draft for chapter one should be completed in a week, and I wrote down the specific date. Not wanting to fail myself, I wrote each day and met the deadline. This tells us that discipline is also key in setting goals. So, with objective one completed, I moved on to the next. This helped me to feel accomplished, capable and I was not overwhelmed. I had never written a book before, so I was on new grounds.

My encouragement is, after having a dream or coming up with an idea, the next best thing to do is to make it visible, whether through a journal or vision board. **Tony Robbins** rightly said, "Setting goals is the first step to turning the invisible into visible." It now becomes a personal declaration of your intentions. The prolific and ever strategic **Les Brown** encourages us to review our goals twice daily in order to be focused on achieving them. Keep the plan fresh in your mind, turn it into a motivation to live. As **Robert H. Schuller** said, "Goals are not only absolutely necessary to motivate us. They are essential to really keep us alive."

Lesson 3: Prepare a plan of action. Do not write it down and forget it. A written dream cannot get up

Activate To Achieve

and perform for you. This was a mistake I made, so I detested setting goals.

"A dream written down with a date becomes a goal. A goal broken down into steps becomes a plan. A plan backed by action makes your dreams come true." —**Greg S. Reid**

Preparing daily action plans of where you will go and on which day, who you will meet to help with what, and what time a specific part of the plan needs to be accomplished will make life easier.

Lesson 4: Share your idea with your biggest cheerleader. We all have someone or a group of persons who have our best interest at heart or are always there to give support and a listening ear. This person or persons also check on your progress when you share a dream. If you do not have any such person, you need to check your circle. It is also very important that you be careful who you share with because they may just steal the idea.

Lesson 5: Be disciplined; go through the steps in lesson 3 and put those plans into action. The person you said you would meet, ensure you schedule a time and be there, be prepared to discuss and expand your resources. The date you have set to accomplish the task, ensure you put in continuous and consistent work to meet the deadline. I accomplished this book by following those five steps. **Proverbs 21:5 (ESV) says,** "The plans of the diligent lead surely to abundance…" and **Jim Rohn** said it just as well as the good book, "Discipline is the bridge between goals and accomplishments." When you make a plan regarding a goal, the work you put in is what you will reap.

Chapter Three

Positioning Yourself

"Success is where preparation and opportunity meet." —Bobby Unser

Luke 19:1-10 tells the story of a wealthy man by the name of Zacchaeus, who sought to see Jesus. There was a great crowd preventing Zacchaeus from seeing Jesus, so he ran ahead of the crowd and climbed a sycamore tree. Jesus had not met Zacchaeus prior to that day, but when He reached the tree, He looked up, addressed him, and visited his home. When Jesus visited his home, Zacchaeus made a presentation of his plans which was to give away a portion of his wealth. Zacchaeus acted on those plans immediately, and through this act, Jesus granted him salvation.

Shackeria D. Mesquita

It would not hurt many of us, whether Christian or not, to have a Zacchaeus mentality; actively putting ourselves in a position to reap. He had a goal, which was to see Jesus. Many other persons had that same goal, but instead of giving up, he came up with a plan and acted on it. You are not going to be the only one with an idea, but you cannot throw in the towel and give up. While we all want to be unique, sometimes our uniqueness is not what we come up with but how we came up with it or achieved it. Furthermore, a little competition is sometimes the motivation we need. So, he separated himself from the crowd and climbed a great tree where he would be able to see his target. There are a number of fast-food chains around the world offering the same products but with their own little twist. If our favourite fried chicken place looked and said, "Well, that burger joint does chicken sandwiches; let me stick to just serving plain old chicken," then we would not have the chicken sandwich variety we have today. And guess what? There are a lot of persons who would much rather eat a chicken sandwich prepared at the fried chicken place, over the one made at the burger joint any day of the week. Being innovative does not mean you have to come up with a brand new idea. It also means

Activate To Achieve

being unique in your creation; taking something old and making it new.

It is said that a sycamore tree has a substance that will mess you up if you rest on it. It also grows big, having branches set apart, therefore making it difficult to climb. Zacchaeus looked beyond these obstacles and placed himself in a position where he could see Jesus. Your goal may just be geared towards your passion, but that does not mean you are not going to encounter difficult hurdles. What are you going to do; stop when you encounter negative criticism or minor setbacks? The first step is too big an effort to turn back now. Keep going, be adamant about your goals, and flexible about your methods. Zacchaeus gained some attention from Jesus in that sycamore tree. If you position yourself positively and correctly, the right investor or sponsor will see you. Chances are, you may not need to open your mouth; they may just approach you. When Jesus visited Zacchaeus, he shared his plans and immediately acted on them.

Now, when you approach an investor, potential client or prospective partner, always be prepared to sell your product or brand. Be able to represent in a convincing manner because talk is cheap, but action is powerful. Do you know how good an impression you can make if you approach someone or they approach you regarding your goals, and you are prepared to share and present? Imagine being prepared and presenting in such a way that this person gives an on-spot favourable response, not only from the idea being sold but from your attitude of preparedness and your ability to express yourself.

When Zacchaeus shared his plans and immediately acted on them, he received salvation. Now that is a blessing, one that affords the ability to overcome and endure in our hard times. This story reveals the power of setting a goal, positioning oneself, having the right attitude, and presenting your goals in a convincing manner. The end result is blessings.

The practice of introspection has revealed to me that thoughts can be manifested when we act on them. So I realized the importance of positive thinking over my life, and I became further activated to achieve. It is key to position yourself from in your mind and then make it a reality. If you get up and think or anticipate that your day is going to be bad, then it may just turn out bad after all because you would have placed yourself in that position. **Proverbs** 17:22 (**ESV**) says, *"A joyful heart is good medicine, but a* *crushed spirit dries up the bones."* Being joyful and appreciative of a new day fuels the soul and puts you in a position to overcome daily adversities. You may ask, what about those who get up and go out in good spirits, yet negative things happen? My response is, we have no control over the things that will happen throughout the day, but we can control how we react to the situation. Putting yourself in the right position and with the right people starts from the mind. If you want something really bad, just think about it. Seriously think about it and envision yourself in the position. Pump up your spirit through thoughts of successfully accomplishing that dream. Now that it is possible in your mind, work on the reality. What do I need to achieve this goal? What if I have this, but I do not have that? Figure out how you can obtain it. The next step would be to acknowledge if you can do what is required, if you are willing to learn or if you will need some help because you are not strong in that area. Now, figure out who you can ask for help; put pride aside and ask. Alright, you asked and got no response, what is your next move? Ask again or ask another. If you got a yes, someone will help, so now you need to focus and play your part. That was a discussion with someone who would have possibly given up because of the initial mindset, "It's too hard," "I don't know what to do," and so on.

Shackeria D. Mesquita

Think positive, be positive, and do positive. Activate yourself for what you want, and it will manifest.

Chapter Four

Persistence, Consistency, And Discipline Combo

If you are persistent, you will get it. If you are consistent and disciplined, you will keep it.

On my quest to successfully accomplish my God-given purpose as an Empowerment Influencer, through my roles as an educator, speaker, and youth mentor, I observed that persistence, consistency, and discipline are key ingredients for success. Having acknowledged this, I had to be cognizant that success takes time to develop.

Being kicked out of high school made me nervous each time I enrolled in a learning institution or a training session. I feared not making it to the end. I had to work extremely hard to make it by feeding my mentality. I got involved in extra-curricular activities, nation-building projects, serving on the student council, or being the group representative for my entire tenure at college. You see, once I felt I was doing something to help others, I had to tap into what fueled me. Find what works for you and use it to propel you. Helping people gave me a sense of purpose and the need to be where I was. It awakened an intelligence I never knew I had in me. So, being kicked out again or quitting was not an option. That being my mantra, I had to persist.

Persistence is when you have passed one hurdle and you keep going, knowing that there may be another hurdle ahead, but you are going to tackle it. **Galatians 6:9 (ESV)** says, *"And let us not grow weary of doing good, for in due season we will reap, if we do not give up."* If your goal is for personal benefit to help with nation-building or economic growth for your country, then it will require you to keep going even when you are weary. As the Bible says, in due season you will reap.

I listened to my Bishop, C. Everton Thomas, one day, and his message was about being persistent. He made reference to the word obstacle, which he said is made up of two words; obstruction and tackle. For days I thought about his take on the word's origin, and again I did what had become second nature to me: I reflected on my life and great men and women from various walks of life. I then realized that on the journey to accomplishing our goals, most of us, if not all, come across a hindrance, and we have two choices, we either quit or tackle them. As Bishop said, "Obstructions are meant to be tackled." Reader, I just want you to know I tackled mine, and although it was a rough experience, I am glad I did.

Another part of my strategy was being consistent. For me, this meant unwavering dedication to accomplishing any task. This worked for me and yielded positive results. At teachers' college, I served as a student leader for four consecutive years. Yes, the high school dropout was on a new level. Being a reflective practitioner, I made the best of what worked for me, and I paid attention to what my constituent respected about me. I continued with those traits and worked on what I needed to, while exercising persistence. As such, I was repeatedly voted for, and the ranks also evolved. I began by leading the batch I started with and ended as president leading the entire student body. According to **Tony Robbins,** *"It is not what we do once that shapes our lives, it is what we do consistently."* For me, being consistent paid off.

The final part of the strategy was crucial for the academic part of my college life. I was never a book worm and paying attention to an entire lecture was tedious. I had to dig deep within and muster the courage needed to face my biggest enemy, Mr. Procrastination himself. I had to be disciplined. When I felt like I did not want to do anything, I got up and did them anyway. I had to remember my WHY, and I would remember my father's advice: "Prove him wrong." I also had to trick my brain by taking monitored breaks. So when Mr. Procrastination came to ask, "Aren't you bored?" I was already on a break, eating whole-grained cereals and watching a video that would end by the time my alarm sounded.

Proverbs 13:4 (ESV) tells us, *"The soul of the sluggard craves and gets nothing, while the soul of the diligent is richly supplied."* Having a goal is one thing, but if it is not acted on, then you will have nothing to reap.

> "Self-discipline is about controlling your desires and impulses while staying focused on what needs to get done to achieve your goal." —**Adam Sicinski**

My goal was to become an educator, but I had a fear of not making it through the training process; I needed to conquer the fear. I do not think I conquered it; I believe I successfully tricked the part of my mind that housed the fear. It was a dangerous move, and I would not recommend it if you lack discipline, do not know your limits, or are unsure of your end goals. I went and had fun, but I remembered the prize of obtaining my degree in education. I knew when I had enough, and I was not afraid of saying bye to my company and get back to my WHY.

Fear is like an annoying person who makes a comment that causes you to doubt yourself. However, when it seems like you are up to no good, it is silent. So I tackled my situation by silencing my fear. It does not stay quiet though; I am writing this book, and I feel fearful. But blessed am I to be disciplined to get back to working hard and accomplishing what I set out to do.

My level of persistence, consistency, and discipline were fueled by passion. It is said that working hard for something you do not care about is called stress, while working hard for something you love is called passion. During those four years I was never stressed about the process; I was worried about my mentality. Like many others, when you come face to face with your fears, it is either fight or flight. I would not say I fought or ran away; it was more like some sidestepping. I also experienced anxiousness because I was excited. I was thrilled; success looked, felt, and tasted sweet. I did not want just a taste, I wanted a nice fat slice, and I earned it. Becoming activated made me hungry, and it taught me to survive the storm. Safe to say, it is not so bad to outsmart your fears whichever way you can, and work hard for what you want.

Chapter Five

Focus

"Focus on being productive instead of busy." —Tim Ferris

Keeping your eyes on the prize is a must in order to achieve success. You are going to encounter trials and errors, but you have to keep the vision alive. When you are faced with trying situations, it is your responsibility to keep it together. The road to success, in some cases, is like going through a tunnel. As you enter, things are going to seem dark and never-ending. **Mark Twain** says, *"You can't depend on your eyes when your imagination is out of focus."* Imagination takes place in the head, which means the mind is at work again. If you cannot see the light at the end of the tunnel from inside your mind, then even with your natural eyes wide open, it will be nowhere in sight.

The prolific Jamaican scholar, **Aubrey Stewart,** says *"S-square is the equation that is behind many successful and even unsuccessful people."* S-square, he says, stands for self and surrounding. Now that you are in this tunnel, what is *self* telling you? Is it saying you are going to make it, or you are not going to make it? Is it saying this is hard, or are you prepared for this? Now, what your mind tells you and your attitude's reaction, will determine if you quit or tackle. So, remember to train your mind to be positive. It is at this point you really have to keep it together.

The ***surroundings*** within that tunnel are literally dark and may seem never-ending. This may have a negative effect on you, but the darkness in the tunnel will not last forever. It promises light at the end. Have faith that you will make it to the end. Faith is things hoped for, not those seen; I would rather have hope than nothing.

It is also important to train your vision to block out self-doubt and what the people around you say. Do not become submerged in a surrounding that does not promise fruitful rewards.

"Stay focused on your goals, your peace and your happiness. Don't waste your time on anything that doesn't contribute to your growth." —**Author Unknown**

Do not become one with the darkness in the tunnel; if nothing else, be the light so those who doubt you will see that it can be done.

Proverbs 4:25 (ESV) tells us, *"Let your eyes look directly forward and your gaze be straight before you."* Distractions are going to come in both internal and external forces. That congregation in your head may rise up and ask, "Are you prepared for the responsibility that comes with this newfound success?" Or someone who you did not ask for an opinion may tell you about a friend who tried and was unsuccessful. Do not listen to them; this is your race to run, not theirs. Even if you give them a listening ear, get a kick out of silencing them by asking, "Why did it not work out for their friend?" Chances are they cannot give a reason because they did not run the race or do not have a clue as to what it takes to run the race. I am sure you are familiar with the saying, *"The race is not to the swift but who endures till the end."*

I encourage you to remember why you started and look at the prize. Remember how far you are coming from and look at the prize. All of this distraction is because you are meters away from the tunnel's exit. Have you ever watched a football match? The audience can be very abusive towards the opposing team; that is a known tactic for distraction. Some people do not know the power of their words, but now that you know, it is a form of distraction. Whether they mean it or not, YOU owe it to yourself to finish what you started.

Another aspect of being focused is paying attention to details. There were times when I felt so eager to get things done because I was excited. It is not such a bad thing to be excited about your task or purpose. If you love what you do, it makes the doing worth it. What you need to be careful of is being overly excited to the point where you miss steps and produce the work or present yourself with major glitches. You may come across as being incompetent or mediocre. Focus on the task with keen eyes, review your work, practice and even get a trusted second eye or ears.

While I was finishing up my bachelors, I had my research paper to complete, and I was excited about my study. There were difficult aspects of putting the data together, but the raw data collected intrigued me, and I wanted to share. I could not wait for my assigned research advisor to read through and ask me questions. Questions came, but the simple mistakes I made dampened my spirit a little. My advisor had my best interest at heart. I recognized that and I worked with her and, at the end of the day, I got an **A**. That was just one example out of the many experiences I have had. I am sure if you think about it, you have had some too.

Whenever I lose an opportunity, do not get a call back, or someone pointed out a flaw in my presentation, I always returned to trusty reflection. This helps me to recognize that I was not focused or I moved too fast and missed a significant part of the puzzle which affected the situation/opportunity. You have to be careful on this journey. **2 Timothy 2:15 (NIV)** tells us, *"Do your best to present yourself to God as one approved, a worker who has no need to be ashamed, rightly handling the word of truth."* While your boss, potential partner, or sponsor is not God, do your best to make a great impression. Handling yourself well erases potential embarrassment. There are going to be trials and errors on the success journey; however, you do not want to come across as being mediocre. Your trials, and especially your errors, are lessons and should remain only as lessons. In other words, your trials and lessons should not serve as a hammer for self-inflicted wounds. If you can spot the errors before your big show, that would be great. Keep those trials and errors in your archive as a reminder for the next time, but do not make those become a part of your brand or, worse, become self-sabotaging weapons. So, while you focus on the prize, pay attention to the process and pathway.

Chapter Six

Reflection

"Knowing yourself is the beginning of wisdom." — Aristotle

Have you ever thought about your judgments or ideas? Have you ever been in a position of doubt or uncertainty and consulted your mind affirmations? Well, according to **Positive Psychology Program**, you are normal. All you are doing is reflecting. Introspection or reflecting is a type of mental exercise that helped me to grow and develop by looking inside rather than outside, and it can help you too. This goes back to training and trusting your mind, and leaving the world as a second option for motivation or solution. You may ask others first, but still consult your mind and make your decision from the best solution, which may be your confidant or yourself. Sometimes you may be surprised at how much you learn from your own thoughts. Sometimes your thoughts are better solutions than your confidant's.

"Your visions will become clear only when you can look into your own heart. Who looks outside, dreams; who looks inside, awakes." —**C G. Jung**

Reflecting is, by far, my favourite exercise. Mental health is important to me, having been diagnosed with chronic depression at the age of seventeen. After receiving the help I needed, I made sure to keep my mind fit and feed myself a balanced diet through the Word of God and great motivational men and women. With that, I believe I can take on my God-given purpose, plus more.

Reflection is an exercise that can also function as a mental checklist of the things done. After you have completed a stage of work or the actual task, think about the process and identify what worked and what did not. **James 1:22 (ESV)** tells us, *"But be doers of the word, and not hearers only, deceiving yourself."* Do not just think about the thing and leave it. There needs to be some form of action. If you completed a task and followed up with a session of reflection where the mind revealed what did not work throughout the process, ensure that you make a mental note of it. If you fail to do this, not highlighting it as a "DON'T" and storing it in your trials and error archive, there is a chance you may make that same mistake again. As said before, you cannot make your errors become a part of the brand you have created.

As mentioned in chapter five, focus encourages us to pay attention. Sometimes when looking straight ahead, things get under our feet, and they can be detrimental as small as they are. When you reflect during the process, especially before making the final touches, you can pick up those things that slipped through, find the missing piece of the puzzle; find a concept that does not reflect you or the brand, and make the necessary adjustments.

Chapter Seven

How To Self-Introspect

Enhancing our ability to understand ourselves and our motivations and learning more about our own values help us to take the power away from the distractions of our modern, fast-paced life, and bring our focus back where it belongs. —**Wood 2013**

There is a right and wrong way of doing self-reflection. The main factor boils down to what you are feeding your mind. Even when you feed your mind with positivity, it can distribute negativity. You now have to be quick to stop it before it is fully processed, believed, and acted on. There is a thing called EGO, the part of the mind that thinks it does not need anyone; it distinguishes itself from others in an unbearable way. This is different from trusting your mind and leaving the views of others as a second option. The ego portion of the mind makes the host feel offended by correction and views that are not similar to those revealed by our subconscious mind. **Job 6:24 (ESV)** tells us, *"Teach me, and I will be silent, make me understand how I have gone astray."* A person who trusts his or her mind, sits and pencils through their ideas first and check with their friends later, mainly for confirmation or a second opinion. This person either accepts the opinion or refuses the opinion of others and moves on without hard feelings and will not hesitate to seek their opinion again. The reality is, we will not know everything, and we need people to bring some visions alive.

From my observation, the worst way to reflect is trying to only figure out the **whys** and not so much the **whats**. I remember when starting on my reflective journey, I would ask a lot of "why" questions. Why did this not work? Why are you like that? Why did my mother not want me? I would get a negative response, and it would push me into depression. For example, I lost a competition, and I asked myself, why did I lose? My mind responded, "Either you were not good enough, or the judges were lame." So, there I was, putting myself down or blaming someone else for my failure. This is not only because I was asking "why" questions, but it was also the result of what I used to feed my mind; negativity, self-doubt.

Another time I failed at something, and I asked, what went wrong? My mind revealed that I was not focused, and so some key information was left off, or I did not prepare myself enough. Again it is not just because I asked "what" questions, but my mind had been transformed by this, and it forced me to look deeper. So now I was able to answer the "what" question in a positive way. Do you see the difference between the why and what? Your why may give you a positive response though. I just wanted to share my experience.

One of the best ways to reflect, based on my experience, is through self-evaluation, self-reflective questions, and prompts, such as, have I done anything lately worth remembering? Using ten words, describe yourself or how you would want to be described.

The second way I reflect is through positive affirmations. I write my own and say them aloud in front of the mirror or I listen to those downloaded on the internet before I start my day, after devotion, of course.

The third way I reflect is through a vision board. I love art and craft; making a collage happens to be the only thing I was good at in art class out of all that was taught. A vision board helps me to see a visual representation of the things I love and want for myself; the goals I need to set and achieve. The final way I reflect is by researching self-awareness worksheets and going through them. They may ask questions about my values: What are ten things that are important to me? Or they may ask questions about my perception: How is the public me different from the private me? Things like those help me to really think about myself and refocus where necessary.

The ability to be self-reflective requires will and discipline. It will not be as easy as saying, "I am going to start being reflective." It takes time to develop. You have to give yourself good things to reflect on, and you have to be able to reflect on your negative qualities and see them as lessons and traits that will hinder your success. So, you need to get rid of the negativity and create and maintain the best brand, that is you.

Quotes and Affirmation For Self Activation

I hope these will be a blessing to you as you read and apply yourself to the challenges.

"In every day, there are 1440 minutes. That means we have 1440 daily opportunities to make a positive impact." —Les Brown

How many of those minutes did you use today to make a positive impact?

_____

_____

_____

_____

_____

Challenge: Look at yourself in the mirror and repeat the following affirmations.

1. There is greatness within me.
2. I am good enough.
3. I can do all things through Christ who strengthens me.

Write three of your own:

1. _____

2. _____

3. _____

"By recording your dreams and goals on paper, you set in motion the process of becoming the person you most want to be. Put your future in good hands—your own." —**Mark Victor Hansen**

Activate To Achieve

Where do you see yourself five years from now?

_____

_____

_____

_____

_____

What have you done recently to get you closer to that dream?

_____

_____

_____

_____

_____

Challenge: Write down all you want to achieve and research how to accomplish each.

With that done, believe that you are one step closer. Tackle the most important one; the one that will make you level up, impact your growth and others.

"Position yourself to succeed first by building good relationship with the right people; and then put your efforts and expertise behind that." —Garrison Wynn

Write the name of three persons who have acquired success doing what you are desirous of doing.

1. _____
2. _____
3. _____

Find out how they did it.

Challenge: Look at yourself in the mirror and repeat the following affirmations.

1. I am going to build a relationship that includes God.
2. I am going to build a relationship with the right people.
3. I am willing to take the first needed step to achieve greatness.
4. I will prepare myself for the future I desire.

Write three of your own:

1. _____
   _____
   _____

2. _____
   _____
   _____

3. _____
   _____
   _____

"Dreams get you started; belief, passion, confidence, persistence, consistency and discipline are what will keep you going." —**Brad Taylor**

Let us say you have a dream about a fantastic business idea. Do you believe you can achieve it? Is it aligned with your gifts, talents, or purpose?

_____

_____

How passionate are you about this idea? On a scale of 1-10, 10 being the highest, how confident are you?

Challenge: Look at yourself in the mirror and repeat the following affirmations:

1. There may be obstacles, but I will tackle them.
2. I will continue after crossing each hurdle.
3. When I do not feel like doing anything, I will get up and do it anyway.

Write three of your own:

1. _____
   _____
   _____

2. _____
   _____
   _____

3. _____
   _____
   _____

"Stop getting distracted by the things that have nothing to do with your goals." —**Author Unknown**

Challenge: Look at yourself in the mirror and repeat the following affirmations:
1. I will keep my eyes on the prize.
2. I owe it to myself to accomplish this task.

3. This is my race to run, so I will not listen to my nay-sayers.

Write three of your own:

1. _____

2. _____

3. _____

"It is necessary…for a man to go away by himself…to sit on a rock…and ask, who am I, where have I been and where am I going?" —**Carl Sandburg**

Introspection and reflection are powerful for self-growth.

Who are you? How do you see yourself?

_____

_____

_____

_____

_____

How have you contributed to mankind? What is your purpose?

_____

_____

_____

_____

_____

Where are you now? What can you do to improve your circumstances?

_____

_____

_____

Author's Final Message

My God-given purpose is to empower people to actualize the best version of themselves. My mission is to inspire and motivate as many as I can by living a purpose-driven life and reaching people on various platforms. Too many people are living unfulfilled lives, accomplishing less than they desire or having to settle outside of their true potential, and they have not realized how much they contributed to this through their thoughts.

This book is one of my platforms to reach people. I use this platform to share my journey to success while being as authentic as possible. It includes my setbacks and the mediums I used and still use to propel me along the journey. My aim is not to tell you I have done it so you can do it too, but more so that it can be done. I hope as you become activated, you will see your mind for the force it is and be reflective throughout every aspect of your life.

About The Author

Shackeria Mesquita is an educator, productivity coach, and professional speaker. She is fueled by passion and her God-given purpose to inspire and empower others to be the best version of themselves. Through her messages on "Reflection, The Road To Success," "Rising Above Self-Doubt," "Self-Activate For Success" and "The Power Of Being Youthful And Golden," she has dedicated her time to women and youth empowerment so more women are able to position themselves to serve the world that needs their solutions, and youths can rise above their circumstances and achieve their dreams.

www.ingramcontent.com/pod-product-compliance
Lightning Source LLC
Chambersburg PA
CBHW051706090426
42736CB00013B/2562